W9-CME-033

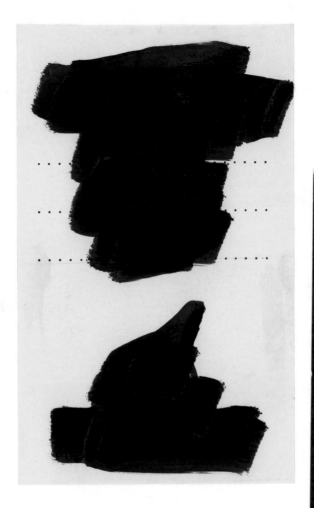

Mardi Gras
A Cajun Country Celebration

Library of Congress Cataloging-in-Publication Data
Hoyt-Goldsmith, Diane.
    Mardi Gras: A Cajun country celebration / by Diane Hoyt-Goldsmith:
    photographs by Lawrence Migdale. – 1st ed.
    p.   cm.
    Summary: Introduces a Louisiana Cajun family and their celebration
  of Mardi Gras including the music, the food, and the costumes.
    Includes index.
    ISBN 0-8234-1184-2
    1. Carnival–Louisiana–Juvenile literature. 2. Cajuns–Louisiana–Social life and customs–Juvenile literature.
3. Louisiana–Social life and customs–Juvenile literature. [1. Mardi Gras. 2. Cajuns. 3. Louisiana.] I. Migdale, Lawrence,
ill. II. Title
GT4210.L8H69 1995   94-42707
394.2'5–dc20   CIP
                                                                             AC

Acknowledgments

This book was made possible by the cooperation and enthusiasm of many people. We would like to thank the Savoy family–Marc, Ann, and their children: Joel, Sarah, Wilson, and Gabie–for sharing their experiences of Mardi Gras with us. They took us to the heart of the Cajun community in Eunice, Louisiana. They shared their food, their music, and their traditions with such generosity that we will never forget the wonderful time we had in their company.

We thank Michelle, Scott, Ashley, and Hayley Ardoin for being such great neighbors and for teaching us the "right" way to make coffee. Another neighbor, Michael Rougeau, was most generous in sharing his experience as a crawfish farmer one bright winter morning.

For their enthusiasm, ideas, and participation, we thank Jane, John, Joseph, and Emily Vidrine; Deborah Helen, Alida, Moise, and Etienne Viator; Linzay, Margaret, and Wendell Young; Philip, Collin, and Daniel Gould and Judith Merriwether; and Michael, Sharon, and Ezra Doucet.

We have very special affection for the young members of the *Gens de la Prairie* band: Joel Savoy and Linzay Young on the fiddle, Karlo Broussard and Horace Trahan on accordion, and Bryson Simoneaux on drums. It was thrilling to be around musicians of such great skill who obviously enjoyed playing together. From them, we gained a real understanding of the way in which the music of the Cajun people and its values are transmitted from generation to generation.

Thanks to Collin Gould and Ezra Doucet for showing us how to enjoy a crawfish boil, Shirley Fisher for her help at the Mardi Gras dance, and to Milton and Marie Adams for sharing some old-time stories and songs with us. We greatly appreciate Curtis Joubert, mayor of Eunice, for the warm welcome he gave us. We appreciate Gilbert LeBlanc and the other Capitaines of the Basile Children's Mardi Gras Run, and Scottie Pousson and the *Point Aux Loups* Playboys who provided the music.

We thank Chris Strachwitz for his help in our research and for putting us in touch with the Savoy family. Thanks to Lorna Mason for her historical insights and to Margery Cuyler for her excellent editorial comments.

If you want to experience a real jam session with some of Louisiana's best Cajun musicians, you are welcome to drop in at the Savoy Music Center any Saturday morning from ten until noon. The store is located on the north side of Highway 190, just east of Eunice. You can't miss it.

If you can't visit Louisiana in person, you can hear some great Cajun music on a number of excellent recordings, both historical and contemporary. You can get recommendations from any of the following sources: Down Home Music Company, 1341 San Pablo Avenue, El Cerrito, CA 94530; Floyd's Record Shop, P.O. Drawer 10, Ville Platte, LA 70586; Roundup Records, 1 Camp Street, Cambridge, MA 02140.

Mardi Gras
A Cajun Country Celebration

by Diane Hoyt-Goldsmith

photographs by Lawrence Migdale

This book is dedicated to
Ari Nathan Migdale,
3/22/94,
and to
Lilian Charlotte Hoyt,
11/10/24 – 1/27/95

Joel is proud of his Cajun ancestors. His favorite fast food is a shrimp po'boy sandwich and his favorite pastime is playing Cajun tunes on his fiddle.

My name is Joel *(joh-ELL)*. I live in a small town called Eunice *(YOO-nis)* in the bayou *(BYE-yoo)* country of Louisiana. Our town is just like any other until it is time to celebrate Mardi Gras *(MAHR-dee GRAH)*. Most of the people who live around Eunice are Cajuns *(CAY-juhns)*, like me. We celebrate Mardi Gras in a special way.

The town of Eunice was established in 1894. Like most of the other towns nearby, it is surrounded by farms.

Joel's sister, Gabie *(gah-BEE)*, feeds her rabbit each morning. They also own two riding horses, chickens and turkeys, a number of cats, and dogs.

Who Are the Cajuns?

Cajun is a term that is short for *Acadiennes (ah-cay-dee-ENZ)*, which is French for "people from Acadia." The Cajuns of today are descendants of French settlers who made a new life for themselves in the early 1600s on the eastern coast of Canada.

The people who moved there were peasants from France. For years, wars had killed thousands of people in their communities and life was very difficult. Many of those who survived decided to move across the Atlantic Ocean to the new colony that France had established in what is now Nova Scotia, New Brunswick, Prince Edward Island, and a part of Maine.

Although settlement began along the shores of the Bay of Fundy as early as 1603, it was many years before the new settlers could plant crops. The land they found was covered with thick forests. Instead of cutting the trees down, the settlers decided to get land for their farms by building dikes to hold the seawater back from the shoreline.

Building dikes was very hard work. Even after completing the walls, the French colonists had to wait three years for the salt to wash out of the soil before they could plant seeds. In the end their efforts paid off. The new settlers created large, fertile farms and a way to earn a good living. They named their new home Acadia, after a place in ancient Greece where people lived a simple, peaceful life.

All of this hard work created strong family ties among the French settlers. Living in France, they had worked long hours in the fields for rich landowners. But in Acadia, they worked for themselves and their own families. They thought of themselves as Acadians, independent people of the frontier. In Acadia, people worked as equals and life was good.

The time of peace and prosperity was short. After only two or three generations, England began to struggle with France for control of Acadian lands. Then in 1713, France surrendered Acadia into British hands.

At first, the British allowed the Acadians to stay on their farms. The new governors asked them to swear allegiance to Britain. When the Acadians refused, British soldiers forced the them to move off their farms. In the years between 1755 and 1765, the Acadians left to find homes in other parts of the world. Their houses and farms were taken over by the English-speaking settlers. The Acadians had to start all over.

Joel and his family live in the same house as his great-great-grandfather did. His ancestors came to Louisiana from Acadia. One of them received an enormous tract of land as a reward for fighting in the Revolutionary War. A large portion of this land grant is owned by Joel's family today.

Some Acadians moved back to France. Others traveled west to live in mainland Canada. Many went to the American colonies of Pennsylvania and Maryland, or to islands in the Caribbean. As the close-knit communities of Acadians scattered, families were split up.

The Acadians who moved to Pennsylvania and Maryland did not feel welcome. Speaking a different language and having different customs made it hard for them to blend in. Even those who returned to France found life to be difficult. In Acadia, they had learned to be free men and women, but in France they were treated little better than slaves.

Throughout the years of their wandering, the Acadians remembered the good life they had made for themselves in the wilderness of Acadia. They never stopped dreaming of finding a "New Acadia" where they could live as they did before.

Finally, beginning in 1765, the Acadians were reunited in Louisiana. Spain, who ruled Louisiana at that time, wanted new settlers to occupy that territory. The Spanish government paid the expenses of Acadians who were living in France to make the long journey across the sea. Many of the other Acadians who had settled in Pennsylvania and Maryland and on the Caribbean islands were eager to be with their families again. They spent all the money they had to get to Louisiana. For all of them, it was a dream come true.

Louisiana had a different climate and landscape from Acadia. It was hot and humid. Many of the crops that thrived in Acadia would not grow in Louisiana. But strong family ties, hard work, and a spirit of independence helped the Acadians to survive in their new environment. They adapted their crops and their lifestyle to fit their new home.

Joel and Gabie like to go to the lake on their family's farm. In the winter, ducks rest there on their way south. In the summer, the lake is a good place to swim and cool off.

8

(Top) Joel helps a neighbor harvest crawfish from his fields. The farmers in this part of Louisiana grow rice one year, then harvest crawfish all the next year on the same land. The fields are surrounded by levees and flooded with a foot or so of water. The farmer's boat has a paddle wheel in the back to propel it through the shallow water. (Right) Joel's brother Wilson helps them unload large sacks of crawfish.

9

Gabie and Sarah enjoy swinging on their front porch. Behind them is an outdoor stairway called a *garçon-nière (gar-sohn-NYAR),* the French term for "boy's staircase." This leads up to the secondfloor attic where the Cajun boys used to sleep. This direct route to their bedroom kept their muddy shoes out of the main house. Nowadays, the stairs make a good fire escape.

Some of our family stories tell about the excitement of those early days. My great-great-grandfather, Valentin, had a spinning wheel factory, a brick kiln, a tannery, and a cotton gin on this property. In those days, all the business transactions were made in gold instead of paper money. The gold had to be deposited in a bank in Opelousas about twenty miles away, because our hometown of Eunice wasn't founded yet. My great-great-grandfather would saddle up his big black stallion and fill the saddlebags with gold. Then he would ask his twelve-year-old son, who was an excellent horseman, to take the gold to the bank.

At that time, there were plenty of bandits who lived in the woods, eager to rob travelers along the trail. But my great-great-grandfather reasoned that robbers wouldn't suspect a small boy to be carrying all that gold. Even so, he told his son not to stop for anyone and not to worry if someone tried to catch up with him. My great-great-grandfather knew that the big black horse could run faster than anything on the prairie. Valentin's son made many successful trips to the bank with his father's gold. That little boy grew up to be my great-grandfather.

In Louisiana, my Acadian ancestors came into contact with tribes of Native Americans as well as with Spanish people, Africans, and Creoles *(CREE-ols).* Creoles are the descendants of early French and Spanish settlers who were born in Louisiana. All of these different people influenced the new "Cajun" identity that my ancestors created.

The Cajuns continued to speak French after they moved to Louisiana. Today, although people my father's age speak French, many of the young people have never learned it.

Over the years, the culture of the Acadians changed. But at the same time, the Cajuns kept many of their old traditions. One of these is the celebration of Mardi Gras.

What Is Mardi Gras?

Mardi Gras is a holiday that takes place on the day before Ash Wednesday, the day that marks the beginning of Lent. Mardi Gras is still celebrated in France, and it is a legal holiday in Florida, Alabama, and eight parishes or counties in Louisiana.

Mardi Gras means "Fat Tuesday" in French. It comes from the medieval custom of parading a fat bull through the streets of Paris on Shrove Tuesday, a time when Christians confessed their sins and were "shriven" or given forgiveness. Early French colonists brought the custom and the celebration from Europe to America in 1765.

When Cajuns celebrate Mardi Gras, they enjoy a tradition that dates back to the Middle Ages. In the country parishes of Louisiana, Mardi Gras is celebrated as a *fête de la quémande* (FET *deh lah kee-*MOND), a begging ritual that began in medieval France.

During the Middle Ages (A.D. 500 – 1500), European society was divided between those who owned land and those who farmed it. As winter became more severe, food was scarce for the poor people who worked in the fields. So they gathered in small groups to walk through the countryside, stopping at castles and manor houses to beg for food from the wealthy. In exchange for something to eat, the people danced and sang and played music.

Today's Mardi Gras celebration in Louisiana's Cajun country has kept its medieval flavor. In the *Courir de Mardi Gras* (COO-REER *deh* MAHR-*dee* GRAH) or Mardi Gras Run, costumed riders travel through the countryside, stopping at farms to ask for donations of a chicken, some sausage, or rice. At the end of the day, the food they have collected is made into a colossal gumbo or stew that is enjoyed by all the people in the community.

Today some people like to make fancy costumes in the Mardi Gras colors: yellow, purple, and green. They use shiny fabric and lots of glitter. But Joel's family still prefers to follow the Cajun tradition. Joel's mother says, "For Cajuns, the more like rags they look, the better."

Joel makes a mask for Mardi Gras from old window-screen material. He cuts the metal mesh into a shape large enough to cover his face. Then he paints on the eyes, nose, and mouth. During Mardi Gras, people try to disguise who they are. That's why Joel adds a mustache to his mask.

Traditional costumes have roots in medieval times, too. Many people wear a tall, pointed cap that is called a *capûchon* (cap-ee-SHON). The pointed hat is similar to those worn by noblemen or jesters in the Middle Ages.

A few weeks before the holiday, there is a frenzy of activity at our house. We get out our old Mardi Gras costumes and try them on to see if they still fit. We like to wear bright colors. Most costumes consist of a pair of pants and a loose-fitting shirt, decorated with rows of fabric cut into a fringe. Some people sew these on, row after row, until the costume is covered with them. I still like to wear the yellow and red costume my father wore when he was my age.

Cajun Music

Cajun music is a very special part of our culture and a part of our everyday life, especially at Mardi Gras time.

Everyone in my family plays an instrument. My mother plays the violin and the accordion. She is also a good singer. My sister Gabie plays the fiddle like I do. Wilson plays the accordion. Both he and my sister Sarah play the piano. Our dad is a wonderful accordion and fiddle player. And he can sing, too.

I was named after my grandfather Joel, who loved music. Although he didn't play an instrument, he invited musicians to his farm nearly every weekend. He boiled crawfish or made a gumbo to feed everyone, and then the visitors would play music until long after midnight.

(Right) Joel and his brother Wilson like to practice together.

(Left) Joel's mother and the other members of her band rehearse some Cajun songs. They meet several times a week in the "buvette" *(boo-VET)*. Built next to the main house before the Civil War, the building is now used as a studio and small guest cottage.

13

Music is the glue that holds the

Joel's father has written sayings on the cabinet doors of his workshop. One of his favorites is: "Music is the glue that holds the Cajun culture together."

My dad tells a story about when he was my age or a little younger. He says, "My own daddy was hard on me. He was good at everything, and when I was small, he made me feel like I couldn't do anything right.

"One day my daddy decided to go dove hunting. He asked if I wanted to go, but I answered, 'No.' I wanted to stay behind to try out a new accordion I got for Christmas.

"Later in the afternoon, when my father came in, he heard accordion music coming from the parlor. He said to my mother, 'Oh, Eli's here.' Eli used to come and play music for my family. But my mama said, 'You go in and see who's playing.' When my daddy saw it was me, his eyes got round with surprise. From then on, it was always 'My son who plays the accordion.' He was so proud of me."

While living in Acadia, the people developed their own style of music from the French songs they brought from the old country. Their music was also influenced by the English and Scots as well as by the Micmac Indians who lived near them.

The Acadians didn't bring many instruments with them to Louisiana. As the English took over their land in Acadia, many of their personal possessions were lost. It is said that the early Cajuns in Louisiana loved music so much, they held dances even *without* instruments. With their voices alone, they were able to make music good enough for dancing.

Accordions are an important part of Cajun music today. When the Acadians first came to Louisiana, the accordion hadn't been invented yet. But German immigrants, who settled in Louisiana in the 1850s, introduced them to it.

Cajun culture together.

Joel uses a template to engrave the brand name "Acadian" onto one of the accordions his father is making.

Then, during World War II (1939-1945), accordion factories in Germany stopped manufacturing instruments and began to make things for the war instead. When my father was a young man, it was hard to find anyone who could repair an accordion or make a new one. He started experimenting and pretty soon he was building instruments of his own. Now he earns a living by making some of the best accordions in the United States. He and my mother also play Cajun music in a band that travels all over the world.

Sometimes I help in my father's workshop. My sister Sarah and I engrave the wood before the accordions are assembled. We help out in the store, too. My father sells instruments of all kinds, as well as musical tapes and CDs. Musicians come from miles around to try out new instruments or to have one fixed. Some come just to talk about music or to ask my father's advice.

Visitors from other parts of the country often ask questions about Cajun music. We tell them it is "homemade," the kind of music we can play every day. Our folk music includes dances, reels, ballads, and songs about every part of life.

Most Cajun songs are sung in French, but the music has been influenced by all the people who have come to live in Louisiana. We have guitars from Spain, fiddles from France, and accordions from Germany. I guess the washboards came from the back porch, and the spoons came from the kitchen.

Like my grandfather, my dad is enthusiastic about Cajun music and is always promoting it. Every Saturday morning, starting at about ten o'clock and continuing until around noon, he holds a jam session in his store.

The Acadian accordions that Joel's father makes are very simple. They have a short keyboard and two bass and chord buttons.

15

Outside the store, a large group of musicians play together with all sorts of instruments. There are accordions, basses, guitars, fiddles, harmonicas, and lots of people singing.

People come from miles around to play their instruments. Musicians of all ages and levels of talent are welcome. Some folks come to dance and sing. Others just watch, listen, and enjoy. There are people who arrive with guitars, fiddles, accordions, mandolins, harmonicas, and basses. Others come to play spoons called *les cuillères* (LAY COO-YEHR) or triangles called *'tit fer* (TIT-FUHR), which is short for *petit fer* and means "little iron." Sometimes people play *frottoirs* (fro-TWARZ), instruments that look like a washboard and are worn over the shoulders as they are played.

16

Although my father holds the jam sessions every Saturday all year round, on Mardi Gras there is usually a huge crowd. Often more than a hundred people come, bringing their own instruments, lawn chairs, coffee, *boudin (boo-DAN)* sausage, and doughnuts to share with the crowd.

My friend Linzay and I like to take up a tune and play it as loud as we can when all the others have stopped for a rest. For Linzay and me, people who have been playing music for a long time are great to be around. We like to listen to them talk about how it was when they were our age.

(Top) Joel participates in a jam session in his father's store. The boy in front is playing a pair of spoons. In the late 1800s, when more sophisticated instruments were not available, a pair of gumbo spoons took the place of the drums and guitars in the rhythm section of Cajun bands.

(Left) Young Cajun musicians like Joel and his friend Linzay rely upon old-timers like Milton Adams for information and inspiration. Milton has been a musician for sixty-three years, and he has a lot to teach the boys. His wife Marie is recording the French ballads that she remembers from her girlhood. Many of these are over three hundred years old.

Making a Gumbo

Eating gumbo is as much a part of Mardi Gras as dressing up and wearing a mask and *capûchon*. My father likes to make a big pot of gumbo with an old family recipe that dates back to his grandmother's time.

Gumbo is a dish that has been influenced by the many cultures that came together in Louisiana. Okra, a vegetable that was once the main ingredient, came from West Africa where it is called *guingombo (GWIN-GUM-boh)*. That is how gumbo got its name. Cayenne *(ky-YEN)*, a red pepper, gives the gumbo its characteristic "hot" spicy flavor.

Although some folks like to make gumbo with seafood, we use chickens from our own farm. My dad adds green peppers and onions. He thickens the soup with a flour and butter or vegetable oil mixture called *roux (ROO)*. We add spicy sausages and *tasso (TAS-soh)*, a Cajun jerky. I like gumbo best when it is served in a bowl over rice with baked sweet potatoes on the side and crisp green onions on top.

Ingredients for Chicken Gumbo

3/4 c. butter or vegetable oil
1 c. white flour
2 1/2 qts. water
1 large chicken, cut into pieces
   with skin and fat removed
2 lbs. lean smoked garlic sausage
   and *tasso,* cut into 2 inch chunks
2 large onions, chopped
1 bell pepper, chopped
Salt, black pepper, and cayenne to taste

Sarah and her father prepare the ingredients for the gumbo.

(Top) Eating a supper of gumbo is a favorite Mardi Gras tradition for Joel's family. (Right) Joel and his family eat King Cake for dessert. Decorated with purple, yellow, and green sugar, it is delicious. Inside one of the slices, a tiny pink plastic baby is hidden. Whoever gets the baby will have good luck, so Gabie is happy to find it in her piece. King Cake is named for the three Magi who visited the baby Jesus in Bethlehem.

19

The Children's Mardi Gras Run

Some communities organize special Children's Mardi Gras runs so kids can participate in and learn about this Cajun tradition. In Basile *(bah-SEEL)*, a town near Eunice, children in bright costumes gather early in the morning. Rather than run or ride on horseback as the adults do, the kids travel to the different neighborhoods in a special trailer decorated for the event.

The *Capîtaines (cah-pee-TEHNS),* dressed in red capes, are in charge. They give the children these instructions before setting out: Honor property. Don't walk on flowers. Don't break anything or mess anything up.

(Top) Following the *Capîtaine,* the children rush to the first house and begin to sing a special Mardi Gras song in French. Joel and his friend Linzay play as the children sing. The kids beg, dancing for the owners of the house.

(Left) Gilbert LeBlanc has been a *Capîtaine* for more than twenty-five years. He uses a dog horn to signal the kids. One blast means "Where are you?" Two mean "I need help." Three mean "Let's go home."

21

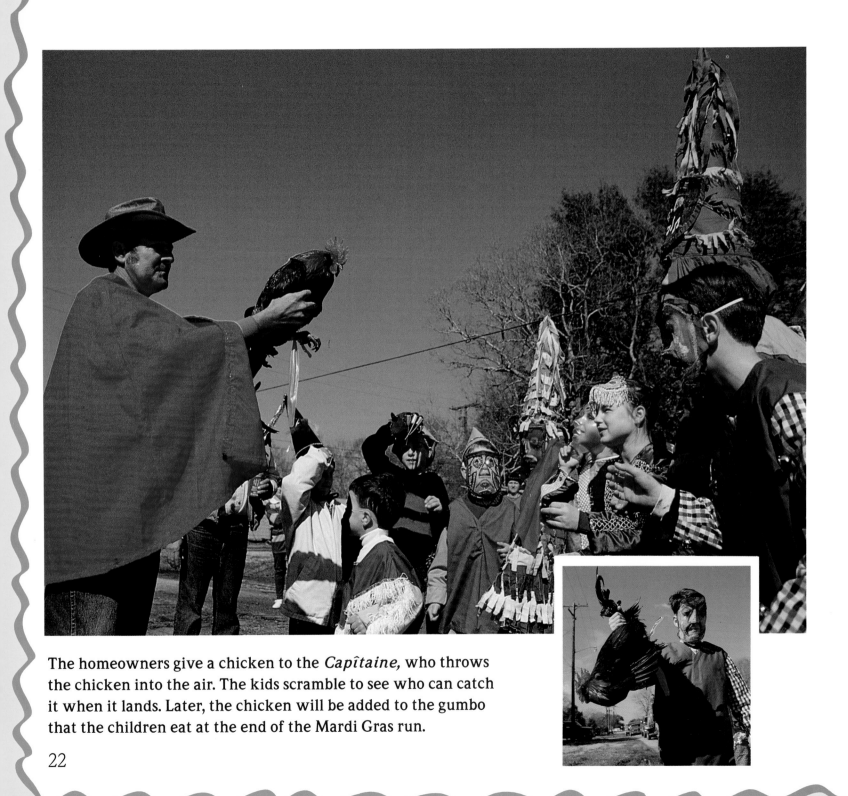

The homeowners give a chicken to the *Capîtaine,* who throws the chicken into the air. The kids scramble to see who can catch it when it lands. Later, the chicken will be added to the gumbo that the children eat at the end of the Mardi Gras run.

22

The last stop on the Children's Mardi Gras Run is Gene's Food Store. The children dance and sing for a donation to add to their gumbo. Gene, the store owner, comes out with a ten-pound bag of rice to contribute to their feast. The children cheer and say, "Thank you."

La Danse de Mardi Gras

by Dewey Balfa

Key of Am
(5th Position)

Les Mar-di Gras ça vient de tout par tout,_____ tout a-len-tour, le tour_ du mo-yeu,_____ ça passe une fois par an_ _ de-man-der la char-i-té._____ Quand-même si c'est une pa-tate, une pa-tate et des_ gra-tons._____

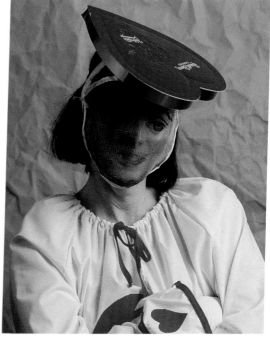

Music and lyrics transcribed by Ann Allen Savoy

Verse 1

Les Mardi Gras ça vient de tout par tout,
Tout alentour, le tour du moyeu,
Ça passe une fois par an
Demander la charité.
Quand même si c'est une patate,
  une patate et des gratons.

The Mardi Gras they come from everywhere,
All around, around the hub,
They pass one time each year
To ask for charity,
Even if it's a sweet potato,
  a sweet potato and some cracklins.

Verse 2

Les Mardi Gras sont dessus un grand voyage,
Tout alentour, le tour du moyeu.
Ça passe une fois par an
Demander la charité,
Quand-même si c'est une poule maigre,
  et trois ou quatre coton mais.

The Mardi Gras are on a big voyage,
All around, around the hub of the wheel,
They pass one time a year,
They ask for charity
Even if it's a skinny chicken,
  and three or four corn cobs.

Verse 3

Capîtaine, Capîtaine, voyage ton flag,
Allons c'ez l'autre voisin,
Demander la charité pour vous-autres,
  vous venez nous rejoindre,
Vous autres vous venez nous rejoindre,
Oui au gumbo ce soir.

Captain, Captain, fly your flag,
Let's go to the other neighbor,
To ask for charity for you all, come join us,
You all come join us,
Yes, at the gumbo tonight.

From "the Balfa Brothers Play More Traditional Music," Swallow LP6019

Courir de Mardi Gras

The Mardi Gras riders come down the road.

The *Capîtaine* asks permission to enter.

The Mardi Gras riders charge the farmhouse.

The main event in Eunice and the surrounding Cajun towns is the *Courir de Mardi Gras,* a time when the adults in the community make their "run" to beg for food to add to the huge community meal at the end of the day. The riders gather just after dawn, dressed in costumes and wearing masks. Many are on horseback, but some ride along on flatbed trucks pulled by farm tractors.

The riders follow the directions of their *Capîtaine.* He sets the rules and is in charge of the riders throughout the run. They travel on the country roads until they reach a farmhouse. Then the *Capîtaine* approaches the house and requests permission for his riders to enter.

They surround the house and begin to dance and sing the Mardi Gras song. Some riders even dance on top of their horses. Others choose dancing partners from among the folks who live in the house. After the performance, the farmer is obliged to "pay" the group with a gift of food. Sometimes it is a sack of rice or some onions. Often it is some sausage, a sack of flour, or money. But the best gift of all is a live chicken.

The riders run after the squawking bird, making everyone laugh. When they capture the chicken, they put it in a burlap sack to take along with them. After more singing and merry-making, the *Capîtaine* sounds his horn, calling the riders to proceed to the next farm.

27

(Top) Joel and his band, *Les Gens de la Prairie,*
entertain the crowds of spectators as they wait
for the Mardi Gras riders to return. The oldest
member of Joel's band is seventeen years old
and the youngest is eleven.

(Right) The kids enjoy a lunch of crawfish
which have been boiled and seasoned with
spices.

At the end of the day, the tired riders enter the town in a joyous parade. They ride past the Liberty Theater, a landmark in Eunice and the scene of many great Cajun music concerts. They have collected enough food to put on a large gumbo feast for themselves and the whole community.

While everybody waits for dinner to cook, they listen to Cajun bands and dance. The riders eat first, and then the whole town joins in. Everyone enjoys the last big party before Lent.

Joel and his sister Gabie walk down the driveway that leads from the road to their house. On some mornings, they can see an armadillo crossing in front of them.

The day after Mardi Gras dawns clear and cold. It is Ash Wednesday and people get up early in the morning. Many go to church where a priest marks a cross of ashes on the foreheads of the worshipers. This is done as a symbol of penitence and purification. The season of Lent has begun.

My father's family has lived in this part of Louisiana for seven generations. For the Cajuns, the way we live, the foods we eat, our language, the music we play, the things we celebrate, all make us feel special and unique. We are Americans, yet we have a style all our own. When we celebrate Mardi Gras, we are celebrating our Cajun history, our music, and our unique identity.

Glossary

Acadia: The territory in Nova Scotia, New Brunswick, Prince Edward Island, and a part of Maine that was settled by French immigrants in 1603-1765.

accordion: An instrument with a bellows, keyboard, and reeds.

bass: *(BACE)* A very large violin-like instrument that stands on the floor while its strings are plucked. Its name comes from the low, bass sounds it produces.

bayou: *(BYE-yoo)* A marshy waterway that is often connected to a lake or river.

boudin: *(boo-DAN)* A sausage made with rice, pork, red and black pepper, salt, and other spices.

buvette: *(boo-VET)* A small building that serves as a pub or "drinkery."

Cajun: *(CAY-juhn)* A shortened term for the French Acadiennes, who settled in Louisiana.

Capîtaine: *(cah-pee-TEHN)* The leader of the Mardi Gras celebration who is responsible for the safety and orderly conduct of the riders.

capûchon: *(cap-ee-SHON)* The tall, pointed hat worn by people during Mardi Gras.

cayenne: *(ky-YEN)* A spicy red-pepper seasoning.

Courir de Mardi Gras: *(COO-REER deh MAHR-dee GRAH)* The French term for the Mardi Gras Run, in which riders travel from farmhouse to farmhouse begging for food while entertaining residents.

cracklins: The crisply fried skin and fat of a hog, also called gratons *(grah-TOHNS)*.

crawfish: *(KRAH-fish)* Also called crayfish and crawdads, these small freshwater shellfish are popular in Cajun cooking.

Creole: *(CREE-ol)* A person born in Louisiana of French or Spanish parents.

les cuillères: *(LAY COO-YEHR)* The French term for "spoons," a percussion instrument in Cajun folk music.

dike: *(dike)* A seawall built from stones and earth to hold back tidal waters.

fête de la quémande: *(FET deh lah kee-MOND)* A French begging procession in the Middle Ages.

fiddle: A folk term for a violin.

frottoirs: *(fro-TWARZ)* A French term for an instrument like a washboard that is worn over the shoulders and played with a pair of bottle openers or spoons.

garçonnière: *(gar-sohn-NYAR)* An outdoor staircase leading to the attic of a Cajun house where the boys slept.

guingombo: *(GWIN-GUM-boh)* A West African term for okra, a green vegetable used in making gumbo.

gumbo: *(GUM-boh)* A stew made of chicken or seafood, onions, peppers, and thickened by roux. Its name comes from *guingombo*, or okra, one of the original ingredients.

King Cake: A cake decorated with colored sugars and eaten on Mardi Gras. In one there is a tiny prize for good luck.

Lent: A period of fasting and repentance for Christians that begins on Ash Wednesday and continues for forty days until Easter.

levee: Walls made of earth built to contain water used to flood farmland.

Magi: The three kings from the East who visited the newborn Jesus in Bethlehem.

medieval: Referring to the Middle Ages (A.D. 500-1500) in Europe.

parish: A county in Louisiana.

roux: *(ROO)* A thickener for gumbo made from flour browned in vegetable oil or butter.

tasso: *(TAS-soh)* A spicy Cajun smoked and dried meat.

template: A pattern used for tracing or cutting a design into another material.

'tit fer: *(TIT-FUHR)* A French term for a triangle made from the tines of an old hay rake and used as an instrument. Those made from old iron tines are said to have the richest sound.

Joel's Favorite Cajun Musicians

I've been lucky to know some of the greatest Louisiana fiddlers. Dennis McGee and Dewey Balfa have been frequent visitors in my home. I was raised hearing their music.

I like Wade Frugé's (Froo-ZHAYS) traditional fiddle style a whole lot, and I liked him as a person. I am proud that he left me one of his fiddles when he died. I hope I'll be able to play as well as he did one day. I enjoy the bluesy feel to his songs. His music is so laid-back but at the same time, unusual and intense.

I also like Michael Doucet's style. He has exciting and interesting ideas that show up in his playing. Michael is a good friend, too.

Ken Smith is another favorite of mine. He stays close to tradition, but his technique is advanced and wonderful. He really impresses me.

Joel plays on a fiddle that belonged to Wade Frugé, a Cajun musician Joel admires.

Index

(Page numbers in *italics* refer to pages with photographs.)